CHINESE VEGETARIAN COOKING

TIGER BOOKS INTERNATIONAL
LONDON

INTRODUCTION

For too many years vegetarianism in the West has suffered from an image of eccentricity and "crankiness", yet a meatless diet has been an accepted and respectable way of eating for centuries in China. For the Chinese, there were two main reasons for forgoing meat. They have always emphasised the strong link between diet and health, whether bodily, mental or spiritual, and two of the country's most influential philosophies, Taosim and Buddhism, recommend vegetarianism for spiritual health. Many more Chinese, however, are vegetarian by necessity, given the frequent scarcity of meat, poultry and fish in the many poor areas of that vast country. Over the years, therefore, the Chinese have developed many delicious meatless dishes to meet their culinary needs, and a complete vegetarian idiom has evolved within their cuisine.

In Chinese cookery a unique blend of quality ingredients, technique and philosophy combine to produce elegant and mouthwatering dishes. The way in which recipes have evolved reflects the principle of harmony that is so important in the Chinese philosophy of life, and each dish must balance taste, texture, aroma and colour. Within each of these qualities, a separate balance must also be achieved. For instance, taste incorporates the six basic flavours of sweet, sour, pungent, hot, salty and spicy, each of which should be both revealed and balanced in the choice of dishes that constitutes a good Chinese meal. Texture is also an important criterion, and dryness should be contrasted with juiciness, and softness and smoothness with crispness.

Add healthy cooking techniques and the Chinese emphasis on attractive presentation to the equation, and the result is a wonderful style of ethnic vegetarian cookery that looks good, tastes good and is good for you. This combination is both difficult to resist and perfect for modern dietary demands and lifestyles. So explore and enjoy the variety of tasty recipes specially compiled for this book, and do your body and your tastebuds a favour!

3380
This edition published in 1993 by Tiger Books International PLC, London
© 1993 CLB Publishing, Godalming, Surrey
Printed and bound in Singapore
All rights reserved.
ISBN 1-85501-352-5

EGGFLOWER SOUP

*The exotic name of this soup is derived from the
appearance of the egg in the soup.*

SERVES 4

400g/14oz can plum tomatoes
1 tbsp light soy sauce
570ml/1 pint vegetable stock
2 eggs, lightly beaten
2 spring onions, chopped finely

1. Drain and chop tomatoes, removing
pips, and reserve juice.

2. Bring soy sauce, tomato juice and stock
to the boil in the wok. Add tomatoes and
half the spring onions, and cook for 2
minutes.

3. Dribble beaten eggs in gradually,
stirring continuously.

4. Serve immediately, sprinkled with
remaining spring onions.

TIME: Preparation takes 10 minutes, cooking takes 10 minutes.

BAMBOO SHOOT SOUP

*A very decorative soup. Beaten egg sifted into the hot
soup gives a very special effect.*

SERVES 4

90g/3oz bamboo shoots, cut into thin
  matchsticks
4 dried Chinese black mushrooms, soaked
  for 15 minutes in warm water
850ml/1½ pints vegetable stock
1 tbsp wine vinegar
2 tbsps light soy sauce
Salt and pepper
½ tsp cornflour, combined with a little
  water
1 egg
10 chives

1. Blanch the bamboo shoots in boiling,
salted water for 3 minutes. Rinse and set
aside to drain.

2. Cook the mushrooms in boiling, salted
water for 10 minutes. Rinse and set aside
to drain.

3. Bring the stock to the boil and add the
bamboo shoots, mushrooms, vinegar, and
soy sauce and season with salt and
pepper to taste. Cook for 10 minutes.

4. Stir in the cornflour and bring the soup
slowly back to the boil.

5. Reduce the heat. Beat the egg
thoroughly. Place the beaten egg in a
sieve and add to the soup by shaking the
sieve back and forth over the hot soup.

6. Add the chives to the soup and serve
piping hot.

TIME: Preparation takes about 5 minutes and cooking takes approximately 30 minutes.

WATCHPOINT: Make sure the soup is boiling hot before adding the beaten egg.

COOK'S TIP: Try to buy fresh chives for this soup, as they have a
much better flavour than dried chives.

WONTON SOUP

*Probably the best-known Chinese soup, this recipe uses
pre-made wonton wrappers for ease of preparation.*

SERVES 6-8

20-24 wonton wrappers
90g/3oz finely minced Chinese mushrooms
2 tbsps chopped Chinese parsley
   (coriander)
3 spring onions, finely chopped
2.5cm/1-inch piece fresh ginger, peeled
   and grated
1 egg, lightly beaten
1.5ltrs/2½ pints vegetable stock
1 tbsp dark soy sauce
Dash sesame oil
Salt and pepper
Chinese parsley or watercress for garnish

1. Place all the wonton wrappers on a
large, flat surface. Mix together the
Chinese mushrooms, chopped parsley,
spring onions and ginger. Brush the edges
of the wrappers lightly with beaten egg.

2. Place a small mound of mixture on one
half of the wrappers and fold the other
half over the top to form a triangle.

3. Press with the fingers to seal the edges
well.

4. Bring the stock to the boil in a large
saucepan. Add the filled wontons and
simmer 5-10 minutes or until they float to
the surface.

5. Add remaining ingredients to the soup,
using only the leaves of the parsley or
watercress for garnish.

TIME: Preparation takes 25-30 minutes, cooking takes about 5-10 minutes.

BUYING GUIDE: Wonton wrappers are sometimes called wonton skins. They are available
in speciality shops, delicatessens and Chinese supermarkets. Chinese parsley is also known
as coriander and is available from greengrocers and supermarkets.

POT STICKER DUMPLINGS

*So called because they are fried in very little oil and
they will stick unless they are brown and crisp
on the bottom before they are steamed.*

MAKES 12

Dumplings
175g/6oz plain flour
½ tsp salt
3 tbsps oil
Boiling water

Filling
100g/4oz finely minced Chinese mushrooms
4 water chestnuts, finely chopped
3 spring onions, finely chopped
½ tsp five spice powder
1 tbsp light soy sauce
1 tsp sugar
1 tsp sesame oil

---

1. Sift the flour and salt into a large bowl and make a well in the centre. Pour in the oil and add enough boiling water to make a pliable dough. Add about 60ml/4 tbsps water at first and begin stirring with a wooden spoon to incorporate the flour gradually. Add more water as necessary. Knead the dough for about 5 minutes and allow to rest for 30 minutes.

2. Divide the dough into 12 pieces and roll each piece out to a circle about 15cm/ 6 inches in diameter.

3. Mix all the filling ingredients together and place a mound of filling on half of each circle. Fold over the top and press the edges together firmly. Roll over the joined edges using a twisting motion and press down to seal.

4. Pour about 2.5mm/⅛ inch of oil in a large frying pan, preferably cast iron. When the oil is hot, add the dumplings flat side down and cook until nicely browned.

5. When the underside is brown, add about 90ml/6 tbsps water to the pan and cover it tightly.

6. Continue cooking gently for about 5 minutes, or until the top surface of dumplings is steamed and appears cooked. Serve immediately.

TIME: Preparation takes about 50 minutes including the standing time for the dough.
Cooking takes about 10-20 minutes.

PREPARATION: The pan used for cooking must have a flat base. Do not use a wok.

WATCHPOINT: Make sure the dumplings are brown and crisp on the bottom before adding the water otherwise they really will be pot stickers!

CANTONESE EGG FU YUNG

*As the name suggests, this dish is from Canton.
However, fu yung dishes are popular in
many other regions of China, too.*

SERVES 2-3

---

5 eggs
1 stick celery, finely shredded
4 Chinese dried mushrooms, soaked in
   boiling water for 5 minutes
60g/2oz bean sprouts
1 small onion, thinly sliced
Pinch salt and pepper
1 tsp dry sherry
Oil for frying

Sauce
1 tbsp cornflour dissolved in 45ml/3 tbsps
   cold water
280ml/½ pint vegetable stock
1 tsp tomato ketchup
1 tbsp soy sauce
Pinch salt and pepper
Dash sesame oil

---

1. Beat the eggs lightly and add the celery.

2. Squeeze all the liquid from the dried mushrooms. Remove the stems and cut the caps into thin slices. Add to the egg mixture along with the bean sprouts and onion. Add a pinch of salt and pepper and the sherry and stir well.

3. Heat a wok or frying pan and pour in about 60ml/4 tbsps oil. When hot, carefully spoon in about 90ml/3 fl oz of the egg mixture.

4. Brown on one side, turn gently over and brown the other side. Remove the cooked patties to a plate and continue until all the mixture is cooked.

5. Combine all the sauce ingredients in a small, heavy-based pan and bring slowly to the boil, stirring continuously until thickened and cleared. Pour the sauce over the Egg Fu Yung to serve.

TIME: Preparation takes 25 minutes, cooking takes about 5 minutes for the patties
and 8 minutes for the sauce.

VARIATION: Fresh mushrooms may be used instead of the dried ones.
Divide mixture in half or in thirds and cook one large patty per person.

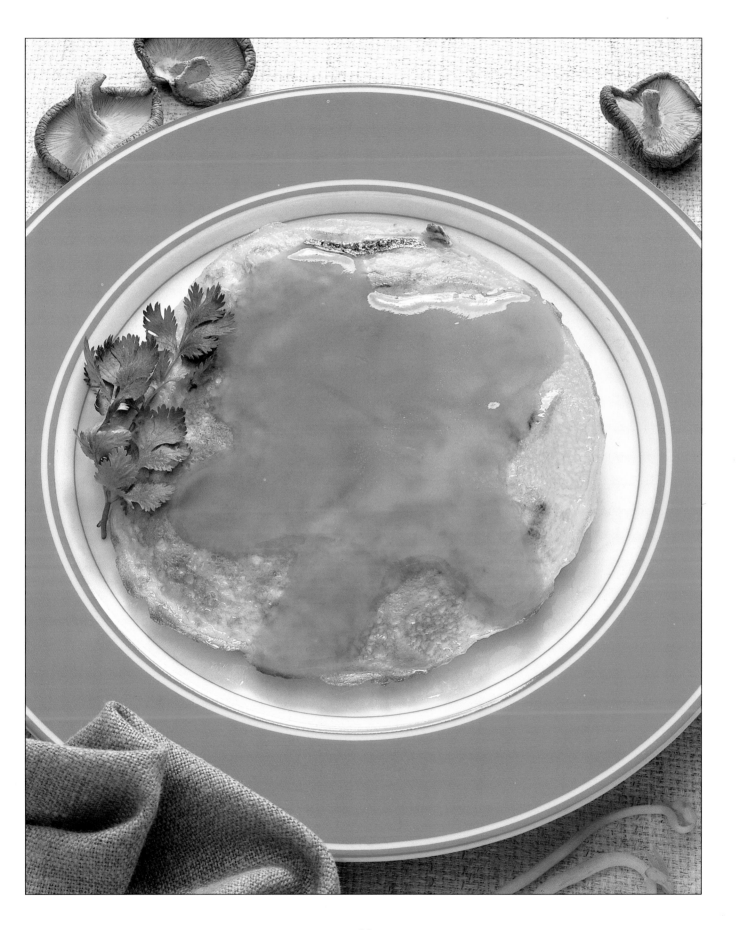

STIR-FRIED CHINESE CABBAGE

Stir-fried Chinese cabbage, courgettes and pepper,
flavoured with sesame oil and soy sauce.

SERVES 4

1 head Chinese cabbage
2 courgettes
2 tbsps oil
1 tsp chopped garlic
1 tbsp chopped red pepper
1 tbsp soy sauce
Salt and pepper
Few drops sesame oil

1. Shred the Chinese cabbage quite finely.

2. Prepare the courgettes, first topping and tailing them and then slicing down the sides, preserving a bit of the flesh with the peel. Slice finely.

3. Heat the oil in a wok, add the Chinese cabbage and garlic and stir-fry for 2 minutes.

4. Add the courgettes, red pepper, soy sauce, salt and pepper. Continue cooking for 3 minutes and serve hot with the sesame oil drizzled on top.

TIME: Preparation takes about 10 minutes and cooking takes approximately 5 minutes.

VARIATION: If you like hot, spicy dishes, add ¼ tsp chilli sauce to the Chinese cabbage.

SERVING IDEA: Cooked in this way, the Chinese cabbage will remain crisp.
If you prefer, cook longer for a softer texture.

BAMBOO SHOOTS WITH GREEN VEGETABLES

A delicious combination of textures and flavours.

SERVES 2

Oil for cooking
225g/8oz chopped spinach, or chopped
    broccoli

Seasoning
100ml/4 fl oz vegetable stock or water
¼ tsp monosodium glutamate (optional)
¼ tsp salt
¼ tsp sugar
100g/4oz bamboo shoots, sliced

Sauce
1 tsp light soy sauce
Pinch monosodium glutamate
1 tsp cornflour
2 tsps water
1 tbsp cooked oil

1. Heat 2 tbsps oil in the wok.

2. Fry the spinach for 2 minutes and add the mixed seasoning ingredients, except the bamboo shoots. Simmer for 1 minute and remove from the wok onto a dish.

3. Heat the wok and add 1 tbsp oil. Add the bamboo shoots and fry for 1-2 minutes.

4. Return the spinach mixture to the wok. Cook for 30 minutes.

5. Mix together the ingredients for the sauce. Add to the wok and cook for 1-2 minutes.

TIME: Preparation takes 10 minutes, cooking takes 10-12 minutes.

COOK'S TIP: Bamboo shoots should always be bought on the day they are to be used as they deteriorate rapidly.

FRIED VEGETABLES WITH GINGER

*Use your imagination with this recipe and adapt it
to whatever greens you can buy.*

SERVES 4-6

1kg/2¼lbs mixed Chinese green
   vegetables (cabbage, spinach, kale,
   broccoli, Chinese leaf etc.)
60g/2oz mange tout
1 tsp bicarbonate of soda
2 tsps sugar
1 tsp salt
2 tbsps oil
2.5cm/1-inch fresh root ginger, peeled and
   shredded
1 green pepper, seeded and diced
1 green or red chilli, sliced into strips

Sauce
2 tsps dark soy sauce
1 tsp sugar
225ml/8 fl oz vegetable stock
2 tsps cornflour
1 tsp five spice powder

To Serve
½ tsp sesame oil
Freshly ground black pepper to taste

1. Cut greens into 7.5cm/3-inch pieces.
Bring a large pan of water to the boil and
add the sugar and salt.

2. Add the mange tout and greens and
cook for 4-5 minutes. Drain green
vegetables and discard water.

3. Add 1 tbsp oil to the vegetables and
keep covered. Heat the remaining oil in
the wok and stir fry the ginger for 1
minute.

4. Add the green pepper and chilli and stir
fry for 10-12 minutes. Add the blended
sauce ingredients and stir well. Simmer
gently for 3-4 minutes.

5. Add the green vegetables and cook for
1 minute. Serve immediately, sprinkled
with sesame oil and pepper.

TIME: Preparation takes 10 minutes, cooking takes 13-15 minutes.

SPECIAL MIXED VEGETABLES

This dish illustrates the basic stir-frying technique for vegetables.

SERVES 4

1 tbsp oil
1 clove garlic, crushed
2.5cm/1-inch piece fresh ginger, sliced
4 Chinese leaves, shredded
60g/2oz flat mushrooms, thinly sliced
60g/2oz bamboo shoots, sliced
3 sticks celery, diagonally sliced
60g/2oz baby corn, cut in half if large
1 small red pepper, cored, seeded and
    thinly sliced
60g/2oz bean sprouts
Salt and pepper
2 tbsps light soy sauce
Dash sesame oil
3 tomatoes, peeled, seeded and quartered

1. Heat the oil in a wok and add the ingredients in the order given, reserving the soy sauce, sesame oil and tomatoes.

2. To make it easier to peel the tomatoes, remove the stems and place in boiling water for 5 seconds.

3. Remove from the boiling water with a draining spoon and place in a bowl of cold water. This will make the peels easier to remove. Cut out the core end using a small sharp knife.

4. Cut the tomatoes in half and then in quarters. Use a teaspoon or a serrated edged knife to remove the seeds and the cores.

5. Cook the vegetables for about 2 minutes. Stir in the soy sauce and sesame oil and add the tomatoes. Heat through for 30 seconds and serve immediately.

TIME: Preparation takes about 25 minutes, cooking takes about 2-3 minutes.

VARIATION: Other vegetables such as broccoli florets, cauliflower florets, mange tout, courgettes or French beans may be used.

SERVING IDEA: Serve with plain or fried rice.

21

AUBERGINES AND PEPPERS SZECHUAN STYLE

Authentic Szechuan food is fiery hot. Outside China, restaurants often tone down the taste for Western palates.

SERVES 4

1 large aubergine
75ml/5 tbsps oil
2 cloves garlic, crushed
2.5cm/1-inch piece fresh ginger, shredded
1 onion, cut into 2.5cm/1-inch pieces
1 small green pepper, seeded, cored and
    cut into 2.5cm/1-inch pieces
1 small red pepper, seeded, cored and cut
    into 2.5cm/1-inch pieces
1 red or green chilli, seeded, cored and
    cut into thin strips
100ml/4fl oz vegetable stock
1 tsp sugar
1 tsp vinegar
Pinch salt and pepper
1 tsp cornflour
1 tbsp soy sauce
Dash sesame oil
Oil for cooking

1. Cut the aubergine in half and score the surface.

2. Sprinkle lightly with salt and leave to drain in a colander or on paper towels for 30 minutes.

3. After 30 minutes, squeeze the aubergine gently to extract any bitter juices and rinse thoroughly under cold water. Pat dry and cut the aubergine into 2.5cm/1-inch cubes.

4. Heat about 45ml/3 tbsps oil in a wok. Add the aubergine and stir-fry for about 4-5 minutes. It may be necessary to add more oil as the aubergine cooks. Remove from the wok and set aside.

5. Reheat the wok and add 30ml/2 tbsps oil. Add the garlic and ginger and stir-fry for 1 minute. Add the onion and stir-fry for 2 minutes. Add the green pepper, red pepper and chilli pepper and stir-fry for 1 minute. Return the aubergine to the wok along with the remaining ingredients.

6. Bring to the boil, stirring constantly, and cook until the sauce thickens and clears. Serve immediately.

TIME: Preparation takes about 30 minutes, cooking takes about 7-8 minutes.

COOK'S TIP: Lightly salting the aubergine will help draw out any bitterness.

SERVING IDEA: Serve with plain or fried rice.

STIR-FRIED TARO AND CARROTS

Taro is a root vegetable which is like potatoes when small.
In this recipe it is cooked with carrots and flavoured with
hoisin sauce to make a delicious side dish.

SERVES 4

450g/1lb taro
1 tbsp oil
225g/8oz carrots, peeled and cut into
    rounds
2 tsps hoisin sauce
100ml/4 fl oz vegetable stock
Salt and pepper

1. Peel the taro and cut it into thin slices.
Put the thin slices back in place. Now cut
the slices into thin strips. Heat the oil in a
work and stir-fry the carrots and taro for 3
minutes, shaking the wok frequently.

2. Add the hoisin sauce and the stock and
continue to cook until slightly
caramelized.

3. Season with salt and pepper and serve
hot. The vegetables should still be quite
crisp.

TIME: Preparation takes about 10 minutes, cooking takes approximately 15-20 minutes.

COOK'S TIP: When stir-frying the taro and carrots, give them time to turn golden brown,
before adding the hoisin sauce.

VARIATION: If you cannot buy taro, use sweet potatoes instead.

VEGETABLE CHOP SUEY

*Stir-fried vegetables, simmered in a wok
with vegetable stock and soy sauce.*

SERVES 4

1 green pepper, seeded
1 red pepper, seeded
1 onion
1 carrot
½ cucumber
1 courgette, thickly peeled and the central
   core discarded
2 cloves garlic
2 tbsps oil
2 tsps sugar
2 tbsps soy sauce
100ml/4 fl oz vegetable stock
Salt and pepper

1. Cut all the vegetables into thin slices.
Prepare the onion by slicing it in half,
then in quarters, and finally in thin, even
slices.

2. Chop the garlic very finely.

3. Heat the oil in a wok and stir-fry the
peppers and garlic for 30 seconds.

4. Add the onion and the carrot and stir-
fry for a further 30 seconds.

5. Add the cucumber and the courgette,
cook for a further 1 minute, stirring and
shaking the wok continuously.

6. Stir in the sugar, soy sauce, stock, salt
and pepper, mixing together evenly.
Simmer until all the ingredients are fully
incorporated. Serve piping hot.

TIME: Preparation takes about 15 minutes and cooking takes approximately 5 minutes.

VARIATION: You could add blanched bean sprouts or sliced,
blanched bamboo shoots to this dish.

COOK'S TIP: If you follow the order given above for the cooking the vegetables,
they will all be cooked but still slightly crisp.

SESAME SPROUT SALAD

Serve as an accompaniment to a hot main dish.

SERVES 4-6

100g/4oz carrots, peeled
1 green pepper
60g/2oz apricots
1 tbsp sesame seeds
225g/8oz beansprouts
4 tbsps French dressing
2 tbsps pineapple juice

1. Cut the carrots into matchsticks.

2. De-seed and slice the pepper thinly.

3. Cut the apricots into slivers.

4. Toast the sesame seeds in a dry pan over a low heat until they are golden brown and give off a delicious aroma.

5. Place the carrots, pepper, apricots and beansprouts in a serving dish.

6. Mix the French dressing with the pineapple juice and fold into the salad.

7. Sprinkle the sesame seeds over the top.

8. Serve at once.

TIME: Preparation takes 10 minutes.

COOK'S TIP: Use beansprouts which are at least 2.5cm/1-inch long for this recipe.

VEGETABLE STIR-FRY

A marvellous blend of Chinese vegetables and nuts,
stir-fried in a little oil and then cooked in an aromatic sauce.

SERVES 4

2 dried lotus roots, soaked overnight in
    water
2 tbsps oil
90g/3oz bean sprouts
½ red pepper, seeded and finely chopped
½ green pepper, seeded and finely
    chopped
½ spring onion, chopped
1 head Chinese cabbage, finely chopped
90g/3oz dried Chinese black mushrooms,
    soaked for 1 hour in warm water
1 courgette, thinly sliced
100g/4oz frozen peas
2 tbsps cashew nuts, roughly chopped
1 tsp sugar
2 tbsps soy sauce
430ml/¾ pint vegetable stock
Salt and pepper

1. Cook the lotus roots in boiling, lightly salted water for 20 minutes. Slice thinly.

2. Heat the oil in a wok and stir-fry, in the following order, the bean sprouts, peppers, onion, Chinese cabbage, lotus root, mushrooms, courgette, peas and cashew nuts.

3. Stir in the sugar, soy sauce and stock.

4. Season with salt and pepper and cook for 30 minutes, stirring frequently.

5. Serve the vegetables slightly drained of the sauce.

TIME: Preparation takes about 10 minutes and cooking takes approximately 35 minutes.

VARIATION: Any type of nut could be used in this recipe, for example walnuts, hazelnuts or almonds.

COOK'S TIP: If time permits, this recipe is even more delicious if the vegetables are stir-fried separately, each cooked vegetable being removed from the wok before continuing with the next. Finish by cooking all the vegetables together for 30 minutes in the vegetable stock as above.

SWEET-SOUR CABBAGE

The perfect refreshing side dish.

SERVES 4

1 medium head white cabbage, about
   900g/2lbs
1 small red chilli pepper (use less if
   desired)
100g/4oz light brown sugar
90ml/3 fl oz rice wine vinegar
30ml/2 tbsps light soy sauce
Salt
45ml/3 tbsps oil

1. Cut the cabbage into 1.25cm/½-inch
slices, discarding the core. Cut the chilli
pepper into thin, short strips, discarding
the seeds.

2. Mix all the ingredients together except
the oil.

3. Pour the oil into a wok and heat for 2
minutes.

4. Add the cabbage and the liquid and
stir-fry for 4-8 minutes depending on how
crunchy you want the cabbage to be.

5. Allow to cool, then transfer to a bowl.
When cold, refrigerate.

TIME: Preparation takes 20 minutes, microwave cooking takes 11-13 minutes.

COOK'S TIP: Vary the amount of sugar and chilli pepper according to your own taste.

SPICY ORIENTAL NOODLES

*Chinese noodles served with lightly cooked
vegetables and a piquant sauce.*

SERVES 4

225g/8oz Chinese noodles (medium
  thickness)
75ml/5 tbsps oil
4 carrots, peeled
225g/8oz broccoli
12 Chinese mushrooms, soaked 30 minutes
1 clove garlic, peeled
4 spring onions, diagonally sliced
1-2 tsps chilli sauce, mild or hot
60ml/4 tbsps soy sauce
60ml/4 tbsps rice wine or dry sherry
2 tsps cornflour

1. Cook noodles in boiling salted water for about 4-5 minutes. Drain well, rinse under hot water to remove starch and drain again. Toss with about 1 tbsp of the oil to prevent sticking.

2. Using a large, sharp knife, slice the carrots thinly on the diagonal.

3. Cut the florets off the stems of the broccoli and divide into even-sized but not too small sections. Slice the stalks thinly on the diagonal. If they seem tough, peel them before slicing.

4. Place the vegetables in boiling water for about 2 minutes to blanch. Drain and rinse under cold water to stop the cooking, and leave to drain dry.

5. Remove and discard the mushroom stems and slice the caps thinly. Set aside with the onions.

6. Heat a wok and add the remaining oil with the garlic clove. Leave the garlic in the pan while the oil heats and then remove it. Add the carrots and broccoli and stir-fry about 1 minute. Add mushrooms and onions and continue to stir-fry, tossing the vegetables in the pan continuously.

7. Combine chilli sauce, soy sauce, wine and cornflour, mixing well. Pour over the vegetables and cook until the sauce clears. Toss with the noodles and heat them through and serve immediately.

TIME: Preparation takes about 25 minutes, cooking takes about 7-8 minutes.

SERVING IDEA: This dish may also be served cold as a salad.

STIR-FRIED RICE WITH PEPPERS

*Long grain rice stir-fried with red and
green peppers, onions and soy sauce.*

SERVES 4

175g/6oz long grain rice
1 tbsp peanut oil
1 onion, chopped
1 green pepper, seeded and cut into small
  pieces
1 red pepper, seeded and cut into small
  pieces
1 tbsp soy sauce
Salt and pepper
1 tsp sesame oil

1. Cook the rice in boiling water, drain
and set aside.

2. Heat the oil in a wok and stir-fry the
onion, add the peppers and fry until
lightly browned.

3. Add the rice to the wok, stir in the soy
sauce and continue cooking until the rice
is heated through completely.

4. Season with salt, pepper and the
sesame oil, and serve.

TIME: Preparation takes 5 minutes and cooking takes approximately 25 minutes.

VARIATION: If you like the strong flavour of sesame oil, stir-fry the vegetables and rice in
this instead of the peanut oil.

Watchpoint: Do not overcook the rice in Step 1, or it will become sticky in Step 3.

PLAIN FRIED RICE

Producing perfect rice is a must
for lovers of Chinese food.

SERVES

450g/1lb Patna or long grain rice
¼ tsp monosodium glutamate
2 tbsps oil
Salt

1. Wash the rice in 4-5 changes of cold water. Drain the rice and put into a large pan or wok. Add sufficient cold water to come 2.5cm/1-inch above the level of the rice. Bring to the boil.

2. Stir once and reduce the heat to simmer. Cover and cook gently for 5-7 minutes until the water has been totally absorbed and the rice is separate and fluffy, with the necessary amount of stickiness to be handled by chopsticks.

3. Spread the rice out on a tray to cool. Sprinkle with the monosodium glutamate. Heat the oil in wok or large frying pan and add the rice. Stir fry for 1-2 minutes.

4. Add salt to taste and stir-fry for a further 1-2 minutes.

TIME: Preparation takes 5 minutes, plus cooling time, cooking takes 10-11 minutes.

NOODLES WITH GINGER AND SOY SAUCE

*Noodles stir-fried with ginger, carrot and courgettes,
then served in an oyster sauce.*

SERVES 4

225g/8oz Chinese noodles
1 carrot
1 courgette
3 slices fresh ginger root
1 spring onion, cut into thin rounds
1 tbsp oil
2 tbsps soy sauce
Salt and pepper

1. Cook the noodles in boiling, salted water, rinse them under cold water, and set aside to drain.

2. Cut the carrot into thin strips. Thickly peel the courgette to include a little of the flesh and cut into thin strips. Discard the centre of the courgette.

3. Peel the fresh ginger root sparingly, but remove any hard parts. Slice thinly, using a potato peeler. Cut the slices into thin strips, using a very sharp knife.

4. Heat the oil in a wok, and stir-fry the spring onion for 10 seconds; add the carrot, courgette and ginger, and stir-fry briefly.

5. Stir in the noodles and cook for 1 minute.

6. Stir in the soy sauce, and continue cooking until heated through. Season with salt and pepper and serve.

TIME: Preparation takes about 15 minutes and cooking takes approximately 15 minutes.

VARIATION: Cook the noodles in vegetable stock instead of salted water to give them extra flavour.

COOK'S TIP: Stir-fry the ginger and the other vegetables very quickly, to avoid browning them. Lower the heat if necessary.

FRIED RICE

*A basic recipe for a traditional Chinese
accompaniment to stir-fried dishes.*

SERVES 6-8

450g/1lb cooked rice, well drained and
  dried
3 tbsps oil
1 egg, beaten
1 tbsp soy sauce
60g/2oz cooked peas
Dash sesame oil
Salt and pepper
2 spring onions, thinly sliced

1. Heat a wok and add the oil. Pour in the
egg and soy sauce and cook until just
beginning to set.

2. Add the rice and peas and stir to coat
with the egg mixture. Allow to cook for
about 3 minutes, stirring continuously.
Add seasoning and sesame oil.

3. Spoon into a serving dish and sprinkle
over the spring onions.

TIME: The rice will take about 10 minutes to cook. Allow at least 20 minutes for it to drain
as dry as possible. The fried rice dish will take about 4 minutes to cook.

COOK'S TIP: The 450g/1lb rice measurement is the cooked weight.

STIR-FRIED STICKY RICE

*Glutinous rice cooked with stir-fried mushrooms,
ginger and spring onions.*

SERVES 4

250g/9oz glutinous rice
2 tbsps oil
2 spring onions, chopped
½ onion, chopped
1 slice fresh ginger root
4 dried Chinese black mushrooms, soaked
   for 15 minutes in warm water, drained
   and sliced
Salt and pepper

1. Wash the rice in plenty of cold water and place it in a sieve. Pour 5½ cups boiling water over the rice.

2. Heat the oil in a wok and fry the spring onions, onion and ginger until golden brown.

3. Add the mushrooms and continue cooking, stirring and shaking the wok frequently.

4. Add the rice and stir well. Pour over enough water to cover the rice by ½ inch.

5. Cover and cook over a moderate heat until there is almost no liquid left. Reduce the heat and continue cooking until all the liquid has been absorbed. This takes approximately 20 minutes in total.

6. Add salt and pepper to taste, remove the slice of ginger, and serve immediately.

TIME: Preparation takes 5 minutes and cooking takes approximately 25 minutes.

VARIATION: Replace the water with vegetable stock to give the rice more flavour.

BUYING GUIDE: If glutinous rice is not available, then long grain white rice can be substituted.

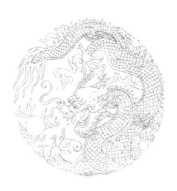

NOODLES WITH PEPPERS AND GINGER

Chinese noodles with stir-fried peppers, ginger and garlic.

SERVES 4

1 red pepper, seeded
1 green pepper, seeded
225g/8oz Chinese noodles
1 tbsp oil
1 tsp chopped fresh ginger root
1 tsp chopped garlic
Salt and pepper

1. Cut the peppers into six pieces.

2. Cut each of these pieces in half, to form slices.

3. Cut each slice into very thin matchsticks.

4. Cook the noodles in boiling, lightly salted water, stirring occasionally so that they do not stick.

5. Drain the noodles in a sieve and pass under cold running water. Set aside to drain.

6. Heat the oil in a wok and stir-fry the peppers, ginger and garlic for 1 minute, stirring continuously.

7. Add the well-drained noodles and stir-fry until the noodles are hot. Season to taste and serve immediately.

TIME: Preparation takes about 15 minutes, and cooking takes approximately 10 minutes.

VARIATION: If you have no fresh ginger root, substitute ground ginger.

WATCHPOINT: If the noodles stick together, run them under hot water until they separate, then drain off the water and continue with Step 7.

51

SPUN FRUITS

*Often called toffee fruits, this sweet consists of fruit
fried in batter and coated with a thin, crisp caramel glaze.*

SERVES 4

Batter
100g/4oz plain flour, sifted
Pinch salt
1 egg
140ml/¼ pint water and milk mixed half
   and half
Oil for deep frying

Caramel Syrup
225g/8oz sugar
3 tbsps water
1 tbsp oil

1 large apple, peeled, cored and cut into
   5cm/2-inch chunks
1 banana, peeled and cut into 2.5cm/
   1-inch pieces
Ice water

1. To prepare the batter, combine all the batter ingredients, except the oil for deep frying, in a liquidizer or food processor and process to blend. Pour into a bowl and dip in the prepared fruit.

2. In a heavy-based saucepan, combine the sugar with the water and oil and cook over very low heat until the sugar dissolves. Bring to the boil and allow to cook rapidly until a pale caramel colour.

3. While the sugar is dissolving heat the oil in a wok and fry the batter-dipped fruit, a few pieces at a time.

4. While the fruit is still hot and crisp use chopsticks or a pair of tongs to dip the fruit into the hot caramel syrups. Stir each piece around to coat evenly.

5. Dip immediately into ice water to harden the syrup and place each piece on a greased dish. Continue cooking all the fruit in the same way.

6. Once the caramel has hardened and the fruit has cooled, transfer to a clean serving plate.

TIME: Preparation takes about 25 minutes, cooking takes from 10-15 minutes.

VARIATION: Lychees may be used. Organisation is very important for the success of this dish. Have the batter ready, syrup prepared, fruit sliced and ice water on hand before beginning.

WATCHPOINT: Watch the syrup carefully and do not allow it to become too brown. This will give a bitter taste to the dish.

ALMOND COOKIES

In China these biscuits are often eaten as a between-meal snack. In Western-style cuisine, they make a good accompaniment to fruit or sorbet.

MAKES 30 COOKIES

100g/4oz butter or margarine
60g/2oz caster sugar
30g/1oz light brown sugar
1 egg, beaten
Almond essence
100g/4oz plain flour
1 tsp baking powder
Pinch salt
30g/1oz ground almonds, blanched or
    unblanched
2 tbsps water
30 whole blanched almonds

1. Cream the butter or margarine together with the two sugars until light and fluffy.

2. Divide the beaten egg in half and add half to the sugar mixture with a few drops of the almond essence and beat until smooth. Reserve the remaining egg for later use. Sift the flour, baking powder and salt into the egg mixture and add the ground almonds. Stir well by hand.

3. Shape the mixture into small balls and place well apart on a lightly greased baking sheet. Flatten slightly and press an almond on to the top of each one.

4. Mix the reserved egg with the water and brush each cookie before baking.

5. Place in a preheated 180°C/350°F/Gas Mark 4 oven and bake for 12-15 minutes. Cookies will be a pale golden colour when done.

TIME: Preparation takes about 10 minutes. If the dough becomes too soft, refrigerate for 10 minutes before shaping. Cooking takes about 12-15 minutes per batch.

COOK'S TIP: Roll the mixture on a floured surface with floured hands to prevent sticking.

WATCHPOINT: Do not over beat once the almonds are added. They will begin to oil and the mixture will become too soft and sticky to shape.

MELON SALAD

*A refreshing fruit salad, which is especially tasty
served after a heavy meal of many courses.*

SERVES 4

1 large cantaloupe melon
1 mango
4 canned lychees
4 large or 8 small strawberries
Lychee syrup from the can

1. Peel and seed the melon and cut into thin slices.

2. Peel and pit the mango and cut into thin slices.

3. Using a melon baller, cut as many balls as possible out the strawberries.

4. Arrange the melon slices evenly on 4 small plates.

5. Spread a layer of mango over the melon. Place a lychee in the centre of each plate and arrange a few strawberry balls around the edges.

6. Divide the lychee syrup evenly between the plates of fruit and chill them in the refrigerator before serving.

TIME: Preparation takes about 30 minutes.

VARIATION: Use a honeydew melon instead of the cantaloupe variety.

COOK'S TIP: This dessert is best served well chilled from the refrigerator, so prepare it several hours in advance of serving.

56

SWEET BEAN WONTONS

Wonton snacks, either sweet or savoury, are another popular tea house treat. Made from prepared wonton wrappers and ready-made bean paste, they couldn't be more simple.

SERVES 6

15 wonton wrappers
225g/8oz sweet red bean paste
1 tbsp cornflour
60ml/4 tbsps cold water
Oil for deep frying
Honey

1. Take wonton wrapper in the palm of your hand and place a little of the red bean paste slightly above the centre.

2. Mix together the cornflour and water and moisten the edge around the filling.

3. Fold over, slightly off centre.

4. Pull the sides together, using the cornflour and water paste to stick the two together.

5. Turn inside out by gently pushing the filled centre.

6. Heat enough oil in a wok for deep-fat frying and when hot, put in 4 of the filled wontons at a time. Cook until crisp and golden and remove to paper towels to drain. Repeat with the remaining filled wontons. Served drizzled with honey.

VARIATION: Add a small amount of grated ginger to the red bean paste for a slight change in flavour. Wontons may also be sprinkled with sugar instead of honey.

BUYING GUIDE: Wontons, wonton wrappers and red bean paste are available in Chinese supermarkets.

CANDIED APPLES

*Candied fruit recipes are popular in Chinese cuisine.
This one is extra special with a rich batter, and
delicious sesame seeds to garnish.*

SERVES 4

3 cooking apples
1150ml/2 pints fresh oil
430ml/¾ pint sesame oil
100g/4oz sugar
1 tbsp toasted sesame seeds

Batter
2 eggs
40g/1½oz flour
40g/1½oz cornflour
Ice water

1. Peel and core the apples and cut into thick circles.

2. Mix the batter ingredients together to make a smooth, thick batter adding water as necessary.

3. Dip the apples in flour and then into the batter.

4. Mix the two oils together and heat to moderate. Deep-fry the apples slices for about 1 minute. Drain and set aside.

5. Heat the oil until it is hot, then fry the apple slices again, for about 40 seconds. This will make them nice and crisp.

6. Pour off most of the oil used to fry the apples, leaving about 3 tablespoons. Add the sugar to this and stir over high heat until the sugar caramelises. Add the apple slices and sesame seeds and stir to coat evenly then remove.

7. Dip the slices into ice cold water to set the syrup before serving.

TIME: Preparation takes about 10 minutes, cooking takes 5 minutes.

DATE DUMPLINGS

*Light and puffy, these steamed date dumplings are
delicious served with a raspberry sauce.*

SERVES 4

150ml/5fl oz water
150ml/5fl oz milk
2 tsps baking powder
1 tbsp sugar
1 pinch salt
400g/14oz plain flour, sieved
15 dates, stoned
1 tbsp ground almonds

1. Mix together the water and the milk.
Incorporate the baking powder, sugar and
salt.

2. Stirring well, incorporate the flour
gradually into the above mixture, forming
it into a ball. You may find it easier to use
your fingers, rather than a spoon.

3. Let the dough rest in a warm place for 1
hour.

4. Place the dates and the almonds in a
food processor and blend until a smooth
paste is formed.

5. On a lightly floured surface, roll out
small lumps of the dough into circles.

6. Place a little of the date mixture in the
centre of each circle. Pull the edges up
over the top, pinching them together well
with your fingers to seal. Roll in your
hands to form small balls.

7. Steam the dumplings for approximately
10 minutes. You may need to do this in
more than one batch.

8. Serve hot or cold.

TIME: Preparation takes about 1 hour 20 minutes and cooking takes
approximately 20 minutes per batch.

SERVING IDEA: Serve the dumplings with a raspberry sauce. Crush fresh raspberries and
add sieved icing sugar to taste. Mix together well and serve.

WATCHPOINT: Make sure that you pinch the edges of the dumplings together
firmly with your fingers before rolling them into balls.

INDEX